William H. Clark

**The Soldier's Offering**

William H. Clark

**The Soldier's Offering**

ISBN/EAN: 9783337306908

Printed in Europe, USA, Canada, Australia, Japan

Cover: Foto ©Suzi / pixelio.de

More available books at **www.hansebooks.com**

THE

# SOLDIER'S OFFERING.

By WILLIAM H. ÇLARK.

———

BOSTON·
1875.

# NOTE.

----

The writer of these desultory sketches and poems, realizing, in part at least, the trying ordeal through which they must pass, if put forth as possessing literary merit and challenging criticism, would remind the reader that they are the production of one who received only the ordinary common-school education : and who, as having served and suffered in the late struggle for the preservation of our glorious Union, asks for a considerate hearing, and deprecates a too severe judgment upon his writings as literary work.

.

# PART I.

/ —

# REMINISCENCES

OF THE

# THIRTY-FOURTH REGIMENT

MASS. VOL. INF.

# CONTENTS.

1*

# CHAPTER I.

## THE FAREWELL.

IT is the afternoon of a summer day, with but little breeze more than enough to gently sway the folds of a new and handsome national flag, which is in full view of the multitude who encompass it. We have taken the reader, in thought, to the spacious and beautiful common in Worcester, on the 15th of August, 1862.

A few words concerning this great gathering; the close attention of all being drawn to the speaker's stand in its centre. Citizens of all classes are here, gazing and listening,

representing the population of the city and
suburbs.   Its inner circles are clothed in the
uniform of their country's service, and stand
in military order.   To them, as a regiment,
through their commander, who is conspicuous
on the stand by his uncovered head and noble
bearing, the flag is being presented: a touch-
ing farewell act of the ladies of Worcester.

It is delivered with fitting words, and now
not only the soldier, but the orator speaks.
Never, while memory lasts, will the picture
be erased from the mind of one, at least;
the central figure, the devoted Wells: so
soon, comparatively, to be the lamented.

The throng breaks, and the regiment
gradually prepares to leave the city for fields
of duty, not to shrink from fields of danger.
Hark! as they slowly recede from sight, and
the clangor of martial music is hushed, can
you not almost distinguish, stealing through
yonder casement where a lonely heart is
thinking of the absent ones, the plaintive
words:

"Thinking no less of them,
  But loving our country the more ;
We've sent them forth to fight for the flag,
  That our fathers before them bore.

Brave boys are they,
  Gone at their country's call ;
And yet, and yet, we cannot forget
  That many brave boys must fall."

# CHAPTER II.

## FUN IN CAMP.

EARY and monotonous indeed, would be many of the days spent in camp by the soldier, did not something crop out of an amusing nature, either in the proper members of the camp or in some of its motley group of followers.

In the Thirty-Fourth Regiment, one such safety-valve was found in a stout, good-natured darkey, who seemed to be the " right hand man " of our regimental sutler.

On one occasion, the " even tenor of his way" was rudely broken in upon, to the great

amusement of the large number who hap-
pened to be in view of that part of the camp
at the time. It seems that a private soldier
of mischievous propensities had been, for
some time, teasing our colored friend by
thrusting a burning twig from the camp fire
into his face; yet, during the ordeal, he had
kept his patience, and only tried to get rid of
his tormentor by entreaties. Suddenly he
turns upon him, forbearance having ceased
to be a virtue in the case, and the two fall
heavily to the ground; Oscar having decidedly the advantage of his enemy, which he as
decidedly keeps. The roar of laughter which
followed this unexpected discomfiture was
probably more pleasant to the ears of Oscar
than to those of his antagonist.

Another little incident in which this sable
philosopher was concerned related to the
legitimate business of the sutler's tent, and
the story was often rehearsed in company E,
and to the amusement of many, by Otis
Hunter, who afterwards, while in the per-

formance of duty as picket·guard at the Shenandoah, near Harper's Ferry, fell through an
opening in the bridge in an unguarded
moment, as was conjectured, and perished by
drowning.   It would seem that at a time when
an unusually large company was gathered in
front of the sutler's tent, one of the "boys,"
whose appetite was more capacious than his
purse, and stronger than his sense of honesty,
had taken advantage of the crowd to secure a
*free lunch*.   Oscar's version of the affair, as
related by poor Hunter, was something like
this: "Well, yer see de feller he comes up
'mongst de crowd, an' says he, I wants a
*fried pie*.   So I takes de fried pie an' hands
it to him, an' looks for de money; but some-
how de feller gits shook up in de crowd, an'
I hav'nt seen *him*, nor de *money*, nor de
*fried pie* since."   This was given with cap-
ital powers of imitation, and never failed to
" bring down the house."

There is something which irresistibly ap-
peals, in many phases of the African character,

to our American sense of humor. At the same time, we discover running through it a vein of sentiment which, blending with the other, dignifies the effect.

" 'Way down upon de Swanee Riber,
    Far, far away ;
Dere's where my heart am turning eber,
    Dere's where de old folks stay.

When I was in de fields a hoeing,
    Near set ob sun ;
So glad to hear de horn a blowing,
    Telling dat de work was done.

O, den de darkies frolic sweetly,
    Banjo in tune ;
Dinah and Phillis dressed so neatly,
    Dance by de big round moon."

## CHAPTER III.

### HARPER'S FERRY.

OR some weeks, the Thirty-Fourth had remained in Washington, D. C., furnishing daily heavy details of neatly equipped men for guard duty; principally to be employed in guarding the Carroll and Old Capitol prisons. During this time, the general soldierly deportment of the rank and file, together with the fine appearance of the regiment on dress parade, attracted much attention and called forth many complimentary expressions from the residents of Washington.

But " marching orders " do not stop to take counsel of their subjects, and on a well-remembered evening in July, 1863, they turned our quiet barracks into a scene of bustle and confusion. A ride of a few hours, over the Baltimore and Ohio Railroad, brought us into the immediate vicinity of Harper's Ferry.

The activity which prevailed throughout our force, on the morning of July 14th, made it evident to all that a movement across the Potomac was intended. All needful preparations having been made, a lively cannonade was opened from the heights above, under cover of which our force embarked in pontoon boats that were near at hand, and crossing, passed through the deserted streets up to the higher ground beyond; dislodging a small body of the enemy which had been holding possession. As the afternoon advanced, a considerable force of cavalry passed through the place, file following file, in a seemingly endless succession, till the eye was wearied with attempting to take in the living current. Our occupation of Harper's Ferry, begun under these circumstances, was destined to continue for many months, with the exception of an occasional brief visit to Martinsburg towards the close of winter.

Perhaps the most notable incident of our service during these months was a trip to Harrisonburg, about one hundred miles into Virginian territory, over that noble production of the road-maker's art, the " Shenandoah Valley turnpike." This splendid avenue of travel deserves more than a passing notice. Its exceedingly hard and smooth surface, composed of finely broken stone, the graded and uniform elevation from either side to the centre, and the long stretch of view in a perfectly straight line, such as may sometimes be obtained on our best surveyed railroad lines; all these combined to call out the admiring comments of those who travelled upon it.

This demonstration, which was success-

fully and safely accomplished, was doubtless
intended as a diversion in favor of the raid
at that time being executed by Gen. Averill,
with his much larger force.

The night scene at Harrisonburg, on the
occasion of commencing our retreat from the
hazardous position in which this comparatively small force was placed, having the
advantage of novelty in our experience, was
one long to be remembered. As soon as
the darkness of night made it practicable,
preparations for a quiet departure were commenced — large fires being lighted and well
supplied with fuel, as though our men were
to pass the night comfortably and without
any demonstration. At the word of com-
mand, silently and swiftly the entire force
withdrew from camp and moved in the direction of Harper's Ferry. Steadily we pressed
on during the entire night, only pausing for
a short halt and rest upon the snow-covered
ground, in the later hours of the night, and
when morning dawned were well on our way

towards the Potomac. Although we were closely followed by a brigade of the enemy, in our rapid and forced march homewards, yet, by the intervention of favorable events, the friendly shadow of the Maryland heights was reached with no loss from our hazardous attempt at " bearding the lion in his den," as our adventure was described by the Richmond Examiner.

Our long stay in this town gave many opportunities for examining its objects of interest, including the engine house, worthy of note as the fortress occupied by John Brown while he held possession, during the brief campaign destined to end so disastrously for those engaged in it. The ruins of armory and other buildings made it very evident that an immense amount of property had been destroyed in the two years in which the spirit of war had held carnival there.

The climate, through the winter months we spent in this place, seemed to suggest some New England locality rather than a part of the "sunny south." Snow storms, and bleak, cold winds, find as congenial a home around those rocky heights as Massachusetts could offer them; at least, such was the impression made upon the mind of the writer. The sublimity and grandeur of Nature's works here well repay any effort required to reach an eligible point of view; but it requires no effort to enable the mind nurtured "beneath New England's sky" to dwell again, in thought, among its native hills.

"Once more, O Mountains of the North, unveil
  Your brows, and lay your cloudy mantles by!
And once more, ere the eyes that seek ye fail,
  Uplift against the blue walls of the sky
Your mighty shapes, and let the sunshine weave
  Its golden net-work in your belting woods,
  Smile down in rainbows from your falling floods
And on your kingly brows at morn and eve
Set crowns of fire! So shall my soul receive
  Haply the secret of your calm and strength,
Your unforgotten beauty interfuse          ,

My common life, your glorious shapes and hues
And sun-dropped splendors at my bidding come,
 Loom vast through dreams, and stretch in billowy
   length
From the sea-level of my lowland home !"

WHITTIER.

# CHAPTER IV.

## THE SKIRMISH.

THE morning of Sunday, October 13, 1863, was a disastrous one for the Ninth Maryland regiment, who were only a few miles distant from our encampment at Harper's Ferry. As the event proved, the enemy, in considerable force, under Gen. Imboden, had made an early and vigorous attack on that regiment at Charlestown, and captured them bodily, in number about three hundred. Every available man of the Thirty-Fourth was promptly called out, and preceded by a battery which was stationed near by, the regiment started in hot pursuit. Often had the wish been expressed that we might see some actual fighting, and at last the wish was to be gratified.

A running fight commenced soon after reaching Charlestown, the battery, which was still in advance, having engaged the enemy just beyond that place. The regiment press hurriedly on, and a few miles of rapid marching bring them into close proximity to the foe, as the shells falling within a short distance from their ranks fully prove. Each company has been assigned the best position allowed by the character of the ground, which is somewhat uneven and obstructed by fences. A lively discharge of musketry is kept up from both sides for a time, but finally ceases. At about this period in the fight, a small body of mounted infantry from the enemy's force charge toward us till but a short space intervenes, and then wheeling easily, soon disappear in the distance.

We afterwards learn that the Springfield muskets of one of our wing companies told with effect on their ranks. The firing has now ceased, and the regiment is ordered to cross the open ground which separates our position from that of the enemy. This is safely accomplished, and it is found that they have again retreated.

Our commanding officer now considers that the pursuit has been pushed far enough, and the order is given to return to Harper's Ferry. Marching and resting alternately, the regiment reach their quarters at a late hour, feeling well satisfied with this first experience of actual fighting. Two of the color corporals, Clark of company K and Gage of company E, have laid down their lives; but they died gloriously, and what matters the form in which death comes, if it finds one in the path of duty,

"Come to the bridal chamber, Death ;
    Come to the mother, when she feels
    For the first time her first-born's breath :

Come when the blessed seals
Which close the pestilence are broke,
And crowded cities wail its stroke ;
Come in Consumption's ghastly form ;
The earthquake shock, the ocean storm ;
Come when the heart beats high and warm,
    With banquet song, and dance, and wine
And thou art terrible : the tear,
The groan, the knell, the pall, the bier,
And all we know, or dream, or fear
    Of agony, are thine.
But to the warrior, when his sword
    Has won the battle for the free,
Thy voice sounds like a prophet's word,
And in its hollow tones are heard
    The thanks of millions yet to be."

HALLECK.

# CHAPTER V.

## BATTLE OF NEWMARKET.

AFTER a march of some hours, our regiment had arrived in the vicinity of Newmarket, Va.; not, however, without an occasional shot being exchanged between the light artillery, which preceded us, and that of the enemy. As we were marched to a position somewhat sheltered by a low ridge, this firing was kept up with vigor. The peculiar tone and expression assumed by our commander, colonel Wells, as he directed our movements, will be remembered by many. "Don't you see

how they are firing at me?" was his demand,
evidently more for its effect on his men than
from any special concern as to his own
safety.

So passed the afternoon of Saturday, May
14, 1864, and the night, a rainy and uncom-
fortable one, settled down upon us; but war
is no respecter of the stillness of night, and
the fact of a foe being close at hand is a
great promoter of uneasiness. Suddenly a
shot is heard, then a volley, and we are
roused up without ceremony; but the alarm
proves nothing serious, being caused by a
small reconnoitering party from the enemy.
We lie down again, all save the watchful
sentinels, and sheltering ourselves from the
rain so far as possible, get what sleep may be
had under the circumstances. A part of the
morning is occupied in putting our arms and
ourselves in good fighting condition, though
this is a difficult matter in some cases; the
rain having reached our muskets to some
extent, in spite of the utmost vigilance.

The quiet is broken by an order to a different position, which order is repeated occasionally during the forenoon, keeping us in motion almost constantly from one point to another. At last, a satisfactory position having been reached, we lie down on our arms for a short time, but soon are ordered to rise and then to load and fire as rapidly as possible. In the meantime, a battery has been stationed on our right, and its guns begin to play on the enemy. After firing several volleys, a charge is ordered, and as we advance, the opposing force comes plainly into view. The yells and cheers accompanying this movement make it almost impossible to hear any order from our superior officers, but we finally comprehend that a "right-about" is ordered. This is executed and we retrace our steps for a short distance, still keeping on a line with the colors, while the continuous cheering of the enemy shows that they fully appreciate their advantage. We now begin to feel seriously the effect of the

heavy fire, both musketry and artillery, which
fills the air with deadly missiles. A promi-
nent field officer is disabled by a severe
wound, and as the enemy press close upon
us, necessarily falls into their hands; while
others, who are less injured, are supported
from the field to receive surgical aid.

The regiment, having reached a good
position, is halted, faced about, and aids in
checking the enemy's advance, much to the
satisfaction of the wounded, who are making
their way to Mt. Jackson, some four miles
distant.   Night falls, and the sounds of battle
are hushed; but this Sabbath day, so dis-
turbed by mortal strife, has proved the last
for many who had cherished hopes of " bright
days yet to be."

" And Ardennes waves above them her green leaves,
　　Dewy with Nature's tear drops, as they pass;
Grieving, if aught inanimate e'er grieves,
　　Over the unreturning brave: alas!
　　Ere evening to be trodden like the grass;
Which now beneath them, but above shall grow

In its next verdure, when this fiery mass
Of living valor, rolling on the foe,
And burning with high hope, shall moulder cold and
        low."

                                                BYRON.

# CHAPTER VI.

## INCIDENTS.

IT will be remembered by some, that at an early period of our regimental history, a fever for enlistment into the regular army prevailed to a certain extent. The causes which produced this state of things are unknown to the writer, but it seems probable that highly colored statements, made by interested parties, as to the relative advantages of one branch of the service over another had been employed.

Col. Wells, as the event proved, felt no sympathy with this movement, and had no idea of quietly looking on while his regiment was depleted in numbers to fill the voracious maw of Uncle Sam. Accordingly, taking his opportunity when the Regiment was out with full ranks, he expressed his views on "the situation" with his usual force and eloquence, and in a manner that held the attention of all to the close. That part of his argument which covered the points of promotion and travel, as nearly as can be recalled, was something like this. "You have been promised opportunities for promotion and travel: as for *travel*, you would have plenty of that, and would have to travel *pretty close to the line*. With regard to promotion in the regular army, there is a regular system of promotion, in which non-commissioned officers only stand a chance of sharing, and they after years of waiting." The address, whether from its sarcasm or its sense, was effectual in curing the uneasiness that had prevailed.

At one time, the young and popular cap-

tain of company E saw fit to celebrate his
birthday by furnishing his men with an unusual treat. A liberal supply of "lager" was
obtained from a neighboring fort, and placed
conveniently in one of the company tents,
with the understanding that all were welcome
to partake. As the evening advanced, a
spirit of jollity naturally prevailed, stimulated
a little, it may be, by the influence of the
Teutonic beverage, and some unusual and
unmilitary noises perhaps, were heard; till
the stentorian voice of orderly sergeant
(since captain) Belser rang out even more
loudly than usual, summoning the company
to fall in for evening roll-call, after which
quiet was restored, and night settled down
peacefully as usual over the camp.

The company, in which occurred the last
incident, numbered among its original members two who were truly of a kindred spirit
and alike in name, though of different nation-
ality — Joseph Smith, whose pranks and
mimicry so often relieved the tiresomeness

of the long march, and Owen Smith, the sturdy son of Erin, equally ready for a fight or a frolic. Once, for some infraction of military discipline in which both were concerned, they were compelled to wear " the wooden shirt," (the name commonly applied to a barrel with an opening cut in the end, through which the culprit's head was passed, the weight of the barrel resting on his shoulders.) Thus equipped, they were obliged to march back and forth before the captain's quarters; yet they were far from being disheartened, but with great merriment performed this unusual sentry duty, assisting each other, in case of any accident, with an almost brotherly regard.

The first mentioned of this pair of intimate friends is believed to have died at Andersonville, Ga. With regard to his comrade, Owen, many years have passed since the writer last beheld his strongly-marked features, and whether the bold Irishman is still in the land of the living is a matter of uncertainty. So drops the curtain over our heroes.

We will close this somewhat disconnected chapter by introducing from the "Atlantic Monthly" for July, 1862, an excellent specimen of soldier-poetry, of which little is said, except that it was "taken from a student-song book, and was probably written in 1814." Not one of the six verses it contains can be spared in reproducing this gem, so replete with a loyal and soldierly spirit. It is unique and perfect in its peculiar line of thought and sentiment : —

### THE CANTEEN.

"Just help me, Lottie, as I spring ;
  My arm is feeble, see, —
I still must have it in a sling ;
  Be softly now with me !
But do not let the canteen slip, —
  Here, take it first, I pray, —
For when that 's broken from my lip,
  All joys will flow away.

' And why for that so anxious ? — pshaw !
    It is not worth a pin :
The common glass, the bit of straw,
    And not a drop within ! '
No matter, Lottie, take it out, —
    'T is past your reckoning :
Yes, look it round and round about, —
    There drank from it — my King !


' By Leipsic near, if you must know, —
    'T was just no children's play, —
A ball hit me a grievous blow,
    And in the crowd I lay ;
Nigh death, they bore me from the scene,
    My garments off they fling,
Yet held I fast by my canteen, —
    There drank from it — my King !          .


For once our ranks in passing through
    He paused, — we saw his face ;
Around us keen the volleys flew,
    He calmly kept his place.
He thirsted, — I could see.it plain,
    And courage took to bring
My old canteen for him to drain, —
    He drank from it — my King !

He touched me on the shoulder here,
  And said, ' I thank thee, friend, —
Thy liquor gives me timely cheer, —
  Thou didst right well intend.'
O'erjoyed at this, I cried aloud,
  ' O comrades, who can bring
Canteen like this to make him proud ?—
  There drank from it — my King ! '

That old canteen shall no one have,
  The best of treasures mine ;
Put it at last upon my grave,
  And under it this line :
' He fought at Leipsic, whom this green
  Is softly covering ;
Best household good was his canteen, —
  There drank from it — his King ! ' "

# CHAPTER VII.

## IN MEMORIAM.

A FEW closing words as a tribute to the honored dead. While referring especially to a few names in this connection, no peculiar honor is claimed for them above the large number of their comrades in other companies whose record is equally honorable; but of those we know best we can, doubtless, best speak.

Brave Christopher Pennell — with a noble ambition leaving his many friends to serve in another field, and falling at last before Petersburg.

Captain William B. Bacon — an able and intrepid soldier, than whom few had brighter prospects of advancement and honor, stricken down at Newmarket, while inspiring his men with his own fearlessness of spirit.

Sergeant Henry B. King — of a gentle and obliging spirit, and beloved by all his comrades; dying on the field of battle, and leaving only the knowledge of his devotion to duty to cheer his youthful and bereaved companion.

The brothers, Dwight and Henry Chickering — noble and promising youths, making the woods ring with the sound of their axes, and their whole-souled laughter, as we prepared to encamp after the day's weary march.

But one more will be particularly mentioned here,* in reference to whom brigade surgeon Clarke used this language, in a letter informing his friends of his death: " he was a brave, conscientious and faithful soldier." And what shall I say of thee, my

---
* Newton H. Clark, of company E.

brother, my faithful friend? Whether in the ordinary duties of the camp, in hours of recreation and of loving communion with friends in the far-distant home, through the medium of the pen, or amid the more fatiguing and exacting experiences of the march, none ever found a truer or more constant companion. Though the snows of many winters have, in their season, robed thy grave with a stainless winding-sheet, yet is thy memory cherished fondly as at first: still shall the flowers of each succeeding summer strew that grave, and the lofty pines of our native state shall furnish thy requiem.

"How sleep the brave, who sink to rest  
By all their country's wishes blest?  
When Spring, with dewy fingers cold,  
Returns to deck their hallowed mould,  
She there shall dress a sweeter sod  
Than Fancy's feet have ever trod.

By fairy hands their knell is rung;  
By forms unseen their dirge is sung;

Here Honor comes, a pilgrim gray
To bless the turf that wraps their clay ;
And Freedom shall awhile repair
To dwell, a weeping hermit, there."

COLLINS.

# PART II.

—

# ORIGINAL POEMS.

# CONTENTS.

3

# MEMORIAL ODE.*

Their's was no common lot,
   Whom we to-day revere ;
No sordid life, no useless work,
   Do we remember here.


Their glorious fame we keep, —
   What precious trust is ours !
" They softly lie and sweetly sleep,"
   Their graves we deck with flowers.

---

\* As originally written.   The first five stanzas being the Ode recited during
the exercises at Town Hall, Holliston, on Decoration Day, May 29th, 1875.

In battle's sharpest strife,
  In heavy, wearing toil,
'Mid bursting shell and whistling ball,
  Or delving in the soil

Of fair Virginia's hills, —
  Whether the trench or field ;
No thought but duty nerved their arm,
  Weapon or spade to wield.

Their narrow, silent beds,
  Where, sunk in peaceful sleep,
These martyred heroes rest from toil,
  As sacred charge we keep.


The sunny clime of France
  Has witnessed oft a scene
Which honors much a valiant name ;
  Nor less *herself*, I ween.

When, as the day returns,
  And, mustered at parade,
A noble corps in silence stands,
  By practised eyes surveyed,

The name is reverent called,
Of one who nobly died ;
And, falling on the attentive ear,
These words are still replied, —

"Died on the honored field ;" *
Fit meed to him who bled, —
And thus would we, in humble lay,
Immortalize our dead.

---

* The last four stanzas refer to a custom, long sustained, in honor of a young French soldier, who had rendered distinguished service, and lost his life in so doing. It is said that whenever the regimental roll was called, the name of this deceased soldier would also be called, and one of his comrades designated for the purpose would respond, "*Died on the field of honor.*"

## AT SUNRISE, JUNE 17, 1875.

.

Ye joyous bells, in merry strain,
Your music yield, again, again,
    Our patriot thoughts to fire ;
That, raised from busy life's routine,
Some higher aims may enter in, —
    Our sluggish souls inspire.

A century has passed, — and now
The change is wondrous — from the brow
    Of yon historic hill,
Whence burst the murderous battle flames,
Where glory rested on the names
    That live in history still,

Shines forth in words of living light
The glories of old Bunker's fight;
    The memories of that day
When PRESCOTT led the deadly strife,
When WARREN's gift, a noble life,
    On Freedom's altar lay.

Ye joyous bells, with loudest peal
Our glorious heritage reveal,
    Its cost, its priceless worth;
Lead us to praise, with loud acclaim,
Our country's God, whose reverend name
    Transcends the names of earth.

# THE "GERMAN."

Hans Spiegler was a Teuton bold,
  Of Faderland extraction;
Phlegmatic, steady, calm and cold —
  An iceberg, he, in action.

His livelihood he fairly earned
  By humble, constant labors;
To know the truth, if you're concerned,
  He *sawed wood* for his neighbors.

'Twas seldom that he ventured in
  The dusk of night to go forth, —
None said *he* sought the haunts of sin,
  With fast young men, &c.

But late one eve, he chanced to pass
    Where music, dancing, drinking, —
Where graceful forms in mirrored glass,
    Set sober Hans to thinking.


His thoughts soon found a vent in speech:
    "*Podshausend! Was ist das?* so —"
His voice the nether regions reached,
    Like notes of deepest basso.


A servant from the basement cried,
    " *The German*, go to thunder," —
But "*Nix furstay*" he still replied,
    With face of puzzled wonder.


And, if you will believe the tale,
    To-day Hans Spiegler gazes,
Unable still to break the spell
    Cast by the "German's" mazes.

# YE SPELLYR.

Full ofte ye spellyr takes hys seate,
  Wythe confidence elate;
Not dreameing to incurre defeate,
  And readye for hys fate : —

But whenne hee takes a lower playse,
  And eates ye humble pye ;
A "proper studie" is hys fayse,
  For "mankinde," youe and I.

# METRICAL LETTER.

*Dear Sister:*
Though the earth should cease its motion,
  *Hornby secede*, and Union lose its power,
Think not to see a wane in my devotion,
  Or be forgotten for a single hour.

The threat, half-uttered, sent in my direction,
  Of causing me to fill a sheet by force —
Made conscience bring to view my late defection,
  And urge my writing as the safest course.

I'm pleased to know that such a patriot fire
  Should be enkindled in our brother's heart;
But while these thoughts do all his soul inspire,
  Let him remember, *Nature yields to Art.*

I don't pretend to call this a quotation,
　　For in a printed page 'twas never seen ;
But for the time I'll take the prompter's station,
　　And bring to view some stubborn facts, I ween.


The drill, the double-quick, the tedious marches,
　　The cold, wet earth his bed, the sky his roof,
Would spoil the beauty of triumphal arches ;
　　He'd wish from battle he had kept aloof.


But, lest you tire of this, my simple measure,
　　I haste, and quickly draw it to a close ;
Wishing our friends much comfort, health and pleasure,
　　And to you, sister, a sweet night's repose.

# TO HENRIETTA.

## ON HER BIRTHDAY.

'Tis said the poor few presents make,
　The rich, of course, do better ; —
Suppose I neither station take,
　What say you, Henrietta?


If I this little token give,
-　I still am much your debtor ;
But if we both some years should live,
　We'll settle, Henrietta.

My heartiest wishes for your good
   Accept, with this short letter,
And may no sorrow ever cloud
   The path of Henrietta.


And when some youth your heart shall hold
   In matrimonial fetter,
I trust you ne'er will say — I'm sold —
   So be it, Henrietta.

# THE THING OF EVEN-TOES.*

There was a thing of Even-toes;
His name was Reynard — sharp his nose —
His eyes were keen — his hunger fierce —
His teeth the toughest fowl could pierce:
     And for this cause,
     By Nature's laws,
The entire feathered race in his immediate vicinity took
special pains to avoid his paws.

The custom was, with Even-toes,
By craft to conquer — not by blows —

---

* Title suggested by Beranger's " King of Yvetot."

A sly old fox was our hero red;
On the choicest fowls he lived, 'twas said:
  And the rascal laughed,
  As their blood he quaffed, —
While all the old chanticleers and dame partlets,
whether shanghais or bantams, were nearly or quite
driven " daft."


This fellow's laugh — 'twas a thing to see —
For a fox *can laugh,* you will all agree —
He would first put on a sardonic grin,
Like an evil sprite, as he mocks at sin ;
  Then he wagged his jaw,
  And the watchers saw
A volley of vulpine cachinnation thence escaping—He !
He ! He ! *Ha ! Ha ! Ha !* HAW ! HAW ! HAW !


"I've a handsome brush," said Even-toes ;
"On my ruby fur the sunlight glows,
When I venture out in the daylight fair —
But at night-time boldly I quit my lair,
  For the silver moon,
  And the night-hawk's croon,
Just stir my blood ; and entirely regardless of the price
of poultry, I walk out with my cousin raccoon."

But the robber's career oft ends in grief ;
And one autumn day, to the great relief
Of the feathered and fatted family fowls ;
And the vengeful joy of his neighbor owls,
Whom he oft had robbed,
As they nightly sobbed ;
(At least, Gray implies that they did,* though it's of no particular consequence in this connection anyway), but as we were about to say, *old Reynard by hunters was mobbed.*

---

* The moping owl doth to the moon complain. —[Gray's " Elegy."

# PART III.

—

# PENCILLINGS.

# A HALF-HOUR WITH TAYLOR.

THOSE whose tastes and preferences in reading agree with those of the writer of this little tribute, will have found a peculiar fascination in the repeated perusal of a poem by Benjamin F. Taylor, one of those names, evidently, which the human heart and mind, appreciating the pure gold of song, will not "willingly let die." It was given in a late number of the "Watchman and Reflector," accredited to "Scribner's Magazine" for April. Its title, "The Psalm Book in the Garret," is

suggestive of the general drift of the poem.
Where all is excellent, there may be diffi-
culty in pointing out special beauties. How
rich in poetic fancy is this stanza: —

> "Ah, richer far than noontide blaze
>    The soft gray silence of the air,
> As if long years of ended days
>    Had garnered all their twilights there."

After the above, which seems to convey
the impression made upon the poet's mind
by the twilight dimness of the secluded
room, and other lines in a similar vein,
comes the discovery of a venerable volume;
which proves to be the talisman to unlock
rich treasures indeed:

> "Where rafters set their cobwebb'd feet
>    Upon the rugged oaken ledge,
> I found a flock of singers sweet,
>    Like snow-bound sparrows in a hedge.
>
> In silk of spider's spinning hid,
>    A long and narrow psalm-book lay" —

And how vividly does the following bring
to view a page of the old psalm-book : —

> " Ah, dotted tribe with ebon heads
>     That climb the slender fence along !
> As black as ink, as thick as weeds,
>     Ye little Africans of song ! "

Here is a touch of tender sentiment :

> " Who wrote upon this page, ' Forget
>     Me Not ? '   These cruel leaves of old
> Have crushed to death a violet —
>     See here its spectre's pallid gold.
>
> A pencilled whisper during prayer
>     Is that poor dim and girlish word : " —

As the poet pursues his examination of
its pages, the old garret seems to be trans-
formed, to his imagination, as by a magician's
wand, into the " old village church," and the
dim twilight of the cramped and darkened
apartment is changed to the daylight glow
of an " olden tyme " sabbath.

> " The village church is builded here ;
>     The twilight turns to afternoon."

Well might the worthies of old afford to worship on uncarpeted floors, so that the reader of the present time may enjoy dwelling once and again upon the beautiful imagery contained in this other couplet: as if the mechanical operation of the carpet-loom were but a transcript or photograph of nature's wondrous working, by which the fairest flowers are produced.

"Thy naked aisle no roses grace
That blossomed at the shuttle's play;" —

The following lines, descriptive of the old-fashioned fugue are especially sweet and graceful, and the quaint imagery introduced in the last four almost unsurpassed:

"The parts strike in with measured grace,
And some thing sweet is everywhere!

As if some warbling brood should build
Of bits of tunes a singing nest,
Each bringing that with which it thrilled
And weaving it with all the rest!"

Desiring to close fittingly, this partial and imperfect view of some of the beauties existing in the poem under consideration, we present one more extract; by no means exhausting the catalogue of gems contained therein.

> " The congregation rise and stand ;
>   ' Old Hundred's ' rolling thunder comes
> In heavy surges, slow and grand,
>   As beats the surf its solemn drums."

# THE VIRGINIA PREACHER.

HE following brief sketch is an attempt to reproduce from memory, as far as is practicable, the leading points of an account given by a distinguished American, many years since, concerning a discourse heard by him in the backwoods of Virginia.

The narrator of the anecdote referred to, was travelling through a thinly settled portion of the state, and came upon a group engaged in listening to one, apparently a minister of the gospel, who was addressing them on what was evidently a weighty and solemn theme. The subject, powerfully handled by the preacher, proved to be the passion, or suffering and death of our Saviour.

As the discourse drew near its close, the preacher entered thoroughly into the spirit of his theme, having the entire congregation completely in sympathy with himself and his subject — the tears flowed freely from many eyes, and sobs burst forth from many hearts, as he portrayed that most deeply affecting scene; one which angels bent down to view with immortal interest, and which concerns so closely every member of our race — the agony and death, upon the cross, of our Lord.

At this point, the narrator, who evidently understood human nature and the art of sacred oratory, seems to have been apprehensive that the preacher would be unable, safely and without shock, to descend from his lofty height, and relieve the deeply wrought feelings of his hearers. But not so — for the almost painful silence which for a few moments succeeded his thrilling description and appeal, was followed by the sublime sentence of Rosseau: "*Socrates* died like a *philosopher*, but *Jesus Christ* like a *God*."

www.ingramcontent.com/pod-product-compliance
Lightning Source LLC
Chambersburg PA
CBHW021526270326
41930CB00008B/1112